THINGS YOU PROBABLY NEVER KNEW YOU

50 Plus Essential Features, Tips and Tweaks for Windows and Mac OS X

SURPRISING TECHNOLOGY SHORTCUTS

BY

Steven Milbrandt

THINGS YOU PROBABLLY NEVER KNEW YOUR COMPUTER COULD DO

SURPRISING TECHNOLOGY SHORTCUTS

PUBLISHED BY

SERENDIPITOUS FINDS PUBLICATIONS

© 2019

50 Mooregate Crescent
Suite 708
Kitchener, Ontario
N2M5G6

DEDICATION

This book is dedicated to the Bayer Family

Linda, Joe, John, Nicole and Jimmy

Thank you all for your friendship, support and kindness.

AND

The Helwigs

Sue, Mike and Jess

A warm family –

Full of good humour and joy

INTRODUCTION

Computers are complex. They are a mix of hardware components, microprocessor chips, a central processing unit, memory, power supply, fans, keyboard and mouse and many other pieces that all work together. They appear deceptively simple because her components are concealed behind plastic and metal boxes, computer screens and keyboards. Even a simple keypress translates to a letter displayed on a monitor is a mystery to many. Most people are simply happy that it works. This complexity both in terms of hardware and software means that many people only employ a fraction of a computer's true capabilities. This book is about what you may not know about the technology you use every day.

Computer hardware is one piece of the puzzle. The computer code that makes programs run and things happen on the screen is the beginning of the real magic that makes the computer the amazing piece of technology that each of us has begun to take for granted every day. It has been estimated that consumers use only 4% of the features available to them within Microsoft Word. It is reasonable to assume that there are many features of Microsoft Word and other programs that are not used to their full potential.

Things you probably never knew your computer could do, and, surprises when things work better than you could ever imagine, is what this book is about. Most of this book will concentrate on Windows 10's often neglected features. Some things referenced here will be largely undocumented and the principal literature and manuals. Some people call surprising features "Easter eggs". Easter eggs are hidden features inserted in hardware and software that can serve to improve speed, personal productivity, enhance functionality or simply to entertain. If you have used Windows for a while, you will probably be aware of some of these features, shortcuts and timesavers, but some will be completely new to you.

There is no one way use this book. No one is saying you must read it from cover to cover. Look through it. Find things that interest you. Try things that may surprise you. One of the best things about technology is that it is always changing and evolving. It is never static. Change is the only constant about most things in life. From the earliest computers that took up entire rooms to the tiniest of computers today that we carry on our wrists and in our pockets, each can do amazing things. Let us look at some of them in these pages. Although we use them every day, and, it is expected that we know how to operate them, many of us muddle through and make mistakes along the way. The people who design the products we use are typically engineers with advanced degrees. They often forget that they are designing products for everyone and that usability and ease-of-use are important.

You probably know a few keyboard shortcuts, but did you know that there are keyboard shortcuts specific to Facebook and twitter? Did you know that you can open a webpage from your toolbar? Did you know that with a few keystrokes you can bring back the hidden administrator account in Windows 10? These are just a few things we will explore in this book. The author hopes you'll find useful and return to it again when you find yourself searching for a quick way to do something or reminder of the specific shortcut. Windows 10, Mac OS, Linux and other operating systems are made up of thousands of lines of code. Each update or revision brings new features or changes to existing ones or the elimination of what now has become outdated and no longer supported. What is current today, may not be relevant five years from now, but it is important to remain as aware of technology as you can, so that you can use it to its fullest potential and be aware of its pitfalls and possible dangers. There is a slogan that is often repeated, "reading is fundamental". Aside from listening and watching, the best way to learn something new is to read. Thank you for reading this book. Your support of the publishing industry in whatever form digital or print is appreciated.

PART ONE

WINDOWS

One of the problems that people face with technology is that there is no one place all the information they need respect to their technology. Sure, there is a lot of information out there especially on the Internet about anything you can ever think to ask on any subject. However, sifting through that information to find relevant, practical and easy to understand information on any given subject is a lot harder. People are often overwhelmed by the choices before them and some, simply give up in frustration. Before we can discuss some things, which will deftly make your life easier, we need to define

Here are some concepts and definitions that you will see throughout this book.

Windows Key or Winkey – is the key with the Windows logo that is often located near the bottom of the keyboard near the alt key. Sometimes there is more than one Windows key on the keyboard, but both perform the same functions.

Alt Key the Alt Key on the keyboard when pressed in combination with the other keys will perform specific functions. Sometimes we represented this way in printed form ALT. The alt key when used in combination with the shift key can also generate special characters the screen.

CONTROL Key - will often be represented with other keys to perform specific functions or tasks on the computer. It will often be represented in this book by the abbreviation CTRL

The Chevron (>) will often represent a choice to follow within a series of instructions such as to go from the system menu to items within that menu or within the same tree or hierarchy of commands. An example might be as follows:

Right click on the desktop select NEW > FOLDER

The line above simply means to right click on the desktop with your mouse and within the window that pops up (the context menu) Select NEW then FOLDER. This will create a new folder on the desktop.

THE START MEMU – This menu is found to the left of the search box on the Windows desktop and can be expanded by clicking on the Windows logo found at the bottom left hand corner in Windows 10. The start menu was removed from Windows 8 and 8.1 in favour of a tiled interface briefly called "tablet mode or metro. However, it was brought back to Windows 10 after many consumers complained about its disappearance.

THE ESCAPE KEY – This key will be represented by the abbreviation ESC

these are a few of the abbreviations and short forms you will find in this book. Others will be explained and represented when they come up and any special considerations such as extra spaces, underlines or specific key presses will be explained in this much detail as possible.

Let us begin with an explanation of the secret start menu. You can find this menu by right clicking on the Windows logo in the bottom left of the Windows 10 screen.

This is a picture of the advanced start menu that you will see when you right click the Windows logo on the left side of the search box in Windows 10. This menu contains many features such as hard drive management (disk management), Task Manager,

Network Connections and other features. Some of these features you may use only occasionally and others you may use often. It is important to be aware that this more advanced menu exists behind the simplified start menu.

Again, you can immediately access it, by right clicking the Windows logo to the left of the search box on the toolbar in Windows 10.

The SHOW DESKTOP BUTTON

This button can be found immediately to the right of the date and time on the toolbar. If you click on this area, you will quickly minimize any open windows that you have open on your desktop.

You can also have windows when you hover your mouse pointer over this area by modifying a setting here:

SETTINGS > PERSONALISATION > TASKBAR > USE PEEK TO PREVIEW THE DESKTOP

GOD MODE

This next tip is nice if you are the kind of person who likes to have all their settings for many Windows 10 features available to you in one convenient place of folder. It has been called "God Mode" by those in the technology community

Here is a picture of this special folder on my Windows 10 desktop

This folder simply displaces a collection of Windows commands and features categorized and all in one convenient place and ready for easy access at any time.

Here is how you can put this special folder on your desktop for quick and easy access to all the most used features and commands in Windows 1o all in one place.

Right click the desktop

Choose NEW > FOLDER

Once the folder is created on your desktop as you need to do is right click the folder, select rename from the popup context menu that appears and rename it with this line of code:

GodMode.{ED7BA470-8E54-465E-825C-99712043E01C}

To enter this mode just double click the folder on your desktop.

ROTATE YOUR SCREEN

This shortcut may appeal to some people. You can rotate your computer screen by pressing

CTRL + ALT + D and any arrow key

For example, try the following combinations

CTRL + ALT + D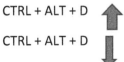

CTRL + ALT + D

CTRL + ALT + D ⬅

CTRL + ALT + D ➡

THE SHAKE FEATURE IN WINDOWS 10

If you have a display full of open bowser windows, you can grab the top corner of the main window that you want to focus on and "shake I t" (move it up and down). This will cause the other windows on your screen to immediately minimize you can concentrate on the window you are immediately working within.

This photo illustrates the shake feature in Windows 10.[1]

The shake feature causes the other windows to be minimized and drop out of sight immediately.

DRAG TO PIN AN OPEN WINDOW TO VARIOUS LOCATIONS ON YOUR COMPUTER SREEN

The above images illustrate two webpages side-by side on my computer screen. If I drag any open window to any of the four corners of my computer screen by taking the top corner, it will

minimize and drop out of sight immediately.

DRAG TO PIN AN OPEN WINDOW TO VARIOUS LOCATIONS ON YOUR COMPUTER SREEN

You can placei two webpages side-by side on my computer screen. If I drag any open window to any of the four corners of my computer screen by taking the top corner, it will

snap into place in that corner of the screen. This is especially good for large screen real estate on big monitors. You can have four different windows open on the screen at any time – one in each corner. This will take up the entire screen with these four different windows that you can see at one time.

For those people who wish they had more monitors attached to the computer but can't because they lack the room or can afford to purchase them, Windows as a solution for you. It is a feature in Windows 10 called virtual desktops. Virtual allow you to separate your open application and windows into virtual desktops on the same screen. To enable virtual desktops, press the ALT + TAB keys. This will bring up the Task View. Task View will separate your open windows and applications.

Drag any of these open windows and applications over to where it says, "New Desktop" on the
screen.

The graphic here shows Victual desktops on my computer monitor. Seen here as "Desktop 1" and "Desktop 2. You could choose to have more than two virtual desktops if system resources and memory permit. Two is simply illustrative of what you would see on your screen.

The author makes no suggestions with respect to computer performance. This is just to show you what a virtual desktop looks like on your monitor.

You can use each virtual desktop to separate applications into various groups or categories. Perhaps you would like to have one virtual desktop with apps you use for work, another with social networks like Facebook, Snapchat or Twitter and still another virtual desktop dedicated to music or audio. Virtual desktops allow the user to simulate having multiple monitors and switch between them rapidly.

NOTE: To switch between virtual desktops use the following key combinations

The WINDOWS KEY + CTRL + LEFT / RIGHT ARROW KEYS

Any long-term use of Windows will remember the hidden administrator account. That was the account that easy could find in the control panel under logins. Using that account, any user who forgot the password could login, usually with credentials: User: ADMINISTATOR Password: admin. The user can then set up an account and thereby gain access to Windows. It turns out, that account is not gone in Windows 10, it is only hidden. A few tweaks in the command line will bring it back. [2]

Here are the steps:

1. In the start menu search box search for CMD
2. Right click the command prompt shortcut that appears in the list of search results and chose "Run as administrator from the context menu that pops up
3. Type the following at the command prompt: net user administrator /active:yes
4. Press ENTER / RETURN
5. This account does not have a password by default so you should add one by typing at the command prompt: net user administrator *

If you have Windows 10 Professional and higher, you can do the same thing in the CONTROL PANEL. Just go to;

CONTROL PANEL > COMPUTER MANAGEMENT > LOCAL USERS AND GROUPS

A. From there, Expand the Users Folder
B. Right click the administrative account
C. Uncheck the box that says "account is disabled"
D. Click OK
E. Right click the administrator account again and chose "Set a password" option

Here is a something else that many people may not be aware. Usually people select text by simply placing the cursor at the beginning of text they want to select, clicking the left mouse button and dragging the cursor across the text until the entire portion they want to select is highlighted. However, there is a much easier way to chose specific portions of text. For example, you can:

A. Select a single word by double clicking on it

B. Select a group of words by double clicking the first while holding down the mouse button, drag it sideways. This way you can chose words in three-word sections
C. Triple click the mouse to select a paragraph

SAVE MULTIPLE ITENS TO THE CLIPBOARD

The clipboard has been around for a long time Windows. It allows you to store things that you copy with commands like CTRL + C. Windows 10 improves this considerably by allowing the user to copy multiple things to clipboard for pasting later. You can set up the cloud clipboard by going to:

SETTINGS > SYSTEM > CLIPBOARD and from there turn on "clipboard History"

you can use this feature to select things you would like to insert into documents. This will help with editing and workflow and improve your well experienced with cutting and pasting and general editing.

CREATE A QUICKLOCK SHORTCUT FOR YOUR COMPUTER

Maybe you have a very busy home environment with lots of people around your computer want a quick way to shut it down with one lock it with one click.

There is a simple way to do this. We can create a quick luck shortcut.

Here is the procedure:

right-click on the desktop

Select NEW > SHORTCUT

in the "Type the location of the Item" box type

rundll.exe user32.dll,LockWorkStation

Click Next

Give the shortcut a name like "Lock PC"

this shortcut will not be visible in your piece you can access it quickly [3]

CREATE YOUR OWN TOOLBARS IN WINDOWS 10

a further way to clean up the desktop is to store things in folders, not on the desktop, but rather in the toolbar shortcut. This way when you click fear when the toolbar, you can easily find the file without it cluttering your desktop.

Essentially, you are creating a folder and placing shortcuts to frequently used programs in that folder.

RIGHT CLICK THE TOOLBAR

CHOSE TOOLBARS > NEW TOOLBAR

BROWSE FOR THAT FOLDER'S SPECIFIC LOCATION AND SELECT THE FOLDER

CLICK THE "SELECT FOLDER" BUTTON

Now a toolbar containing your shortcuts appears to the left of the notification area

Click the Chevrons (>>) beside the toolbar to access them. [4]

IMPROVED SCREEN CAPTURE TOOL IN WINDOWS 10

Those people who appreciate capturing items on their computer screens will like the improved screen capture tool Windows 10. This tool is now called "Snip and Sketch". Bring up this tool with the key combination of SHIFT + WINDOWS KEY + S. The previous version of this was called the "snipping tool"

CONTROL YOUR SMART HOME DEVICES FROM WITHIN WINDOWS 10

Smart home devices such as thermostats, door locks and intelligent light bulbs are fast becoming the "must-have" items of our present society. Everywhere you lock, and new "smart" device enters the market. Most of these devices are not actually smart at all. "Smart" is tech industry jargon for Internet connected. Internet connected devices (Iot) make up one of the fastest-growing segments of consumer electronics today. Many people can not wait to install the newest device in their homes. Many things which you would not expect you made smart such as microwave ovens and refrigerators now come with connectivity to the Internet. In the case of a refrigerator, food items can be monitored for freshness and expiration dates or similar functions.

Whether you are new to the Internet connected device ecosystem or a veteran who purchases everything they can control their home, Windows 10 can be set up control all your devices. To do this, head over to the search box on the desktop and do the following:

A. Search for "Cortana Notebook"

 (This feature brings up a list of suggested tasks for the Microsoft assistant to perform)

B. Click on the "manage skills" tab (at the top of the pop-up window)

C. Scroll down further in that window and click on "Connected Home"

D. Toggle the option in the next window titled "enable connected home"

If you do not see the connected home option in the Cortona notebook settings, it may be necessary to change your computer's LANGUAGE AND REGION settings to the United States. This is because some features are not available in all countries. You can do this by going to the search box on the desktop and typing in "language settings".

You will see something like this for the connected home settings

You will see a lest of possible connected devices such is Honeywell, Hue, ecobee and Nest. Select the device that you would like to configure and follow the manufacture's documentation to do this.

With you have configured all your devices, you can simply ask Cortana to turn on whatever device you want using the parameters set up configured the device(s). Here is important tip. To make interacting with these devices as easy as possible, make sure you give each a distinctive name so there's no confusion about what you want to turn on or connect to respect Cortana.

TURN ON SPEECH RECOGNITION

Along the proliferation of smart devices smart assistant's such as Amazon's Alexa, Google Home, or Apple's Home Pod, interacting with our voices becoming routine. Related to this feature recognition technology. Speech recognition has milked into the operating systems of the major manufacturers for many years. To enable this in Windows 10, simply go to SETTINGS > TIME & LANGUAGE > SPEECH > RELATED SETTINGS then click "Speech Inking and Typing Privacy settings" to enable Microsoft's speech services

Once you enable speeds recognition you can talk instead of type most documents within various programs including Microsoft Word and others were text can be either typed or inserted. This can save you considerable amounts of time, but still requires scrutiny as each recognition software is not perfect.

For more precise dictation, you can use a dedicated dictation software such as Nuance's "Dragon Naturally Speaking". This software is available in several different types such as HOME, PROFESSIOAL AND MEDICAL. Be aware that the more features that are available, the more the product costs to purchase.

Nuance often has sales special discounts. You can find out more about this company's products at

https://shop.nuance.com/store/nuanceus/custom/pbpage.resp-dragon-home-bf-2013-digital

you can also find many dictation apps for the computer and the smart phone available for download. Depending on their complexity, many of these are free.

This author often uses the free website with searching for related software. The website is called Alternative to.

You can find alternatives to many kinds of software at www.alternativeto.org. There is a screen capture above of the alternative to website. Once at that site, just type in the software you're looking to find an alternative for in the search box and look at the various options available on the various platforms such as Windows, Mac and Linux. You can also define your search by paid (Commercial), Freemium (No cost to use with paid options) or free.

Note too that the speech recognition options built in the Windows 10 still require that you adequate for punctuation, spelling variances, and other grammatical changes, but it still means that you will greatly reduce your typing time when you dictate your text.

TURN OFF OR REDUCE NOTIFICATIONS IN WINDOWS

one of the great annoyances of smart phone is the large number of application notifications that can appear on the screen at any given time. Companies compete for your eyeballs and want to do is much as they can to get noticed. This has been true of smart phones for many years. Now the same problem exists in major operating systems like Windows 10 and Apple's Macintosh OS.

Windows 10 tries to address this problem with what it calls "Focus Assist".

Focus assist allows you to customize how you receive notifications in Windows 10.

To enable "focus assist" go to SETTINGS > SYSTEM > FOCUS ASSIST

You can use focus assist to decide which notifications you would like to receive and which ones you would not. Inside this panel could turn off any and all modifications so you're not disturbed or interrupted important tasks.

22

TURN ON "NEARBY SHARING"

nearby sharing is Microsoft's feature which copies Apple's "Air Drop" service. Suppose you want to share a newly created document photograph with another person nearby. You can do this with NEARBY SHARING.

To use the "nearby sharing" feature make sure you have a document or photograph open on your computer. Click the share icon in the toolbar to open another panel, then click "turn on nearby sharing" to see what devices are near you to share to.

You can see the "Nearby Sharing" dialog box in this photograph.

You can use "Nearby Sharing" to share any open document, picture or file after you are granted permission from that person to share it. You must be in fairly proximity to the other person and his or her device to share, but it is a simple and convenient way to share what you are working on with others around you.

CREATE A "HOTKEY" SHORTCUT

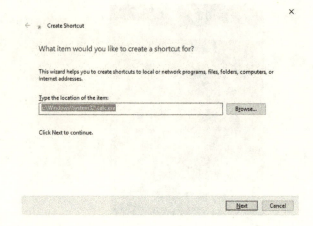

Creating a shortcut Hotkey Graphic

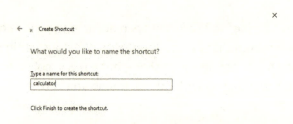

A hotkey is a one key shortcut that you can assign to given tasks or functions within Windows

To create one

RIGHT CLICK THE DESKTOP

CHOSE NEW > SHORTCUT

THEN TYPE THE PROGRAM NAME THAT YOU WANT TO CREATE THE SHORTCUT FOR (SUCH AS calculator.exe)

NAME THE SHORTCUT "Calculator"

CLICK FINISH

RIGHT CLICK THE SHORTCUT ICON AND CHOOSE "PROPERTIES" TO OPEN THE PROPERTIES DIALOG BOX

CLICK THE "Shortcut Key" box to select it

NOW PRESS THE KEY YOU WANT TO USE TO REPRESENT THE SHORTCUT

THE BOX WILL AUTOMATICALLY POPULATE WITH THE CORRECT KEY COMBINATION

For instance, for the letter "c'" key

CLICK APPLY

this means the shortcut for the calculator will now be CTRL + ALT + C

The letter "C" was the key that you assigned in the step above [5]

"Calculator" Properties Dialog box where the shortcut key combination is assigned. See instructions above.

MICROSOFT GAME BAR

Gaming has always been popular both with consoles such as Microsoft's Xbox or the Nintendo 64 and with computers. Many times, gamers believe the gaming experience is much better on the personal computer then on a console because Peter offers more control and options that can be user configured then the clear available on a console.

Microsoft has a feature built into Windows 10 called "Game Bar". This feature turns on the built-in camera mode on the Windows 10 PC. You can turn this on by pressing the WINDOW SKEY + G

Gaming mode does the following:

A. Turns off notifications
B. lets you record / broadcast game play
C. Brings up additional audio controls

this is a quick and convenient way to jump right into the games you enjoy with extra controls and features for according and broadcasting your gameplay as well as the associated audio. You can also search for "Game Bar" in the start menu search box.

This will allow you to set up various keyboard shortcuts for turning the screen capture on as well as the recording timer and microphone ON/OFF.

Speaking of keyboard shortcuts, many people do not know that there are dozens of keyboard shortcuts within every operating system and most programs.

Here are some of the most important that you should know [6]

WINKOWS KEY + A Opens the action center

WINDOWS KEY + I Opens the setting App

WINDOWS KEY + x Launches the power users context menu

WINDOWS KEY + R opens the run dialog box

WINDOWS KEY + TAB launches the task view menu

WINDOWS KEY + RIGHT UP ARROW Moves the active app to the top right

WINDOWS KEY + CONTROL + LEFT OR RIGHT ARROWS moves through your virtual desktops

WINDOWS KEY + CTRL + D Creates a new virtual desktop

WINDOWS KEY + CTRL + F4 Closes a virtual desktop

WINDOWS KEY + S launches the daily weather summary / report

These shortcuts will greatly increase your productivity in the computer because can do in one or two keystrokes my take three or four separate commands to do another way. Familiarize yourself with key Windows shortcuts. Examine shortcuts available in any program you use. Specialized programs may have their own unique shortcuts applicable to the program along. One of the first things a user can do to simplify their life in that only three the manual that comes with or can be downloaded from the Internet, but also to look up available shortcuts within that program.

Often people do not like the default search bar in Windows uses Microsoft's BING for search. There is, however, third-party ways to change this. Here is an example.

If you go to the Chrome Web store at https://chrome.google.com/webstore and download and install the "Chrometana" extension. This extension redirects taskbar searches from the BING search engine to the GOOGLE search engine for example

This means that unless you want to use Bing, you are not required to even within the confines of the taskbar search box. This is not to dictate preferences to you, but to provide you options. Since Google search is the number one search engine on the Internet, chances are you using now, and you want to continue to use it for all your searches. This extension provides one way to do that within the taskbar search box which normally defaults to the Bing search engine.

If you are customizing the taskbar, you also have the option to add the control panel to the start menu. Although the control panel, with its many settings and options is not normally in the start menu as it was in previous versions of Windows, you can easily place it there this way.

A. Search for Control Panel in the desktop search box
B. Right click on the control panel app that comes up in the search box results and select "Pin to Start"

you can also customize Windows and other ways beginning with the lock screen.[7]

Customising or personalizing the lock screen can include adding your own pictures fir lock screen backgrounds

You can also change the colour of the start menu.

There are generally two different types of people who use Windows – those who want to tweak it and make it their own and those who don't want to mess with it and just want to leave it exactly as it is. Often those in the second group live by the adage, "If it is not broke, don't fix it." Whether you are a 'tweaker' or not, the option is there if you chose to exercise it.

One way to really exercise your creative flow is to mark up webpages within the Microsoft Edge browser. This can be a very useful in research and collaboration among workgroups in businesses and research firms that utilize the Internet as the primary search medium. Using this tool, you can write, highlight, edit and even write directly on a webpage. To use this markup feature, follow these steps:

A.   Click on the edit button at the top right of the Edge Browser search bar
B.   A purple bar will appear
C.   There are options along this bar to draw, erase, highlight, make notes and take screen shots

the option to mark up a browser webpage on your desktop means that you can highlight certain things to show others, demonstrate key features and options and provide key elements to any presentation or discussion.

There are many commands and customizations inside Windows 10 designed to boost productivity, minimize downtime, streamline workflow and reduce the time it takes to perform repetitive tasks. If you've been using Windows for a while, you are probably aware of what's called "Keyboard browsing".[8]

Keyboard browsing allows you to browse a document or the Internet using only the keyboard. When this feature is enabled, and soon I need to leave the keyboard and you can speed through a document using only the arrow keys. To launch keyboard browsing:

A.   Go to the (…) three-dot menu
B.   Find SETTINGS > VIEW ADVANCED SETTINGS

C. Enable "Always Use Caret Browsing

When caret (keyboard) browsing is enabled, you can control the flashing cursor (caret), copy and paste text without needing to use your mouse or trackpad.

Caret Browsing is available in the Internet Explorer and Firefox browsers. You can also activate caret browsing after you surf to a browser page where you would like to select text using your keyboard and hit the F7 key.

You can turn keyboard browsing ON / OFF using the F7 key.

DARK MODE

Apple popularized "Dark Mode" and included it in the latest version of OS X Mojave and soon after Microsoft added this feature into Windows 10.

To enable dark mode in the FILE EXPLORER window, go to:

SETTINGS > PERSONALIZATION > COLORS

Then

Scroll to the bottom and chose "Choose your default app mode"

Chose the setting to switch the application mode from light (the default mode) to dark

You could already use / enable dark mode in the start menu, action center and task bar previously, but now Microsoft added dark mode to the File Explorer in a feature update. [9]

this first section of the book showed you some things that you may not have been aware that you could do within Windows, and more specifically, Windows 10. To summarize, the following items and more have been considered:

- Windows 10 desktop personalization
- Windows 10 start menu customization
- Enabling the hidden administrator account in Windows 10
- Using keyboard browsing
- Creating a shortcut to the "God Mode" folder
- Using virtual desktops

- Using Cortana in Windows 10 to control your smart home devices
- Windows 10 application "snap" feature
- Examined the "drag to pin windows" to various locations on the desktop
- Focus assist feature
- Speech recognition settings in Windows 10

And much more

In part two of this book we will examine some more advanced tips and Windows 10 modifications

PART TWO

APPLE

All computers operate in similar ways and their components are alike – CPU, motherboard, graphics card, power supply, monitor, keyboard and mouse. Differences can be seen in the way a particular operating system performs given tasks, how they assign keyboard shortcuts, commands, and the physical appearance of the graphical user interface. Apple Corporation began modestly in the garage of Steve Jobs in southern California. One of the company's slogans was "Think Differently". In this part of the book, let us examine ways that Apple is different from Windows and things that you can do with the Macintosh computer they may not have realized.

First, instead of a Windows Key (the key on a Windows keyboard that kooks like a flying tile), Apple computers have a command key

The command key seen above on a standard apple keyboard has a very distinctive symbol associated with it. Like four intertwined ovals, this key is associated with many different commands and keyboard shortcuts.

"The option key", also found on every Apple keyboard is useful in various commands. For example, if you hold down the option key while closing one open window on a Macintosh computer, all open windows will close. Another example of good use the option key is the force quit command. Its key combination is COMMAND + OPTION + ESC. Whenever a program becomes unresponsive on a Mac, force quit will close that program.

Sometimes on an Apple computer you want to type a special similar character that is not available on the keyboard. For this, you can open the character viewer.

The character viewer allows you select from hundreds of symbols and graphics to insert into any document that you are working on. To get the character viewer on your mac you should do the following on your keyboard.[10]

    A. OPEN SYSTEM PREFERENCES
    B. CLICK "KEYBOARD"
    C. CLICK "INPUT SOURCES"
    D. CLICK ON "Show input menu in system bar"

Once you have the character viewer your screen, simply select where you want to place the character in your document and double click the symbol or character in the viewer that you chose. The symbol will then automatically be placed at that insertion point in your document.

There may also be occasions where you want to take a picture of your Macintosh's computer screen and save that picture for later use it in a document or on a webpage. You take a picture on a Mac you can

PRESS SHIFT + OPTION + 3 – This will take a picture of the entire computer screen
PRESS SHIFT + COMMAND + 4 – This will turn the cursor into a plus sign (+) and you can drag outward in a rectangular shape to take a picture of an area of the screen. If you press shift while you drag, the Mac limits your movements to perfectly vertical or horizontal. If you press the spacebar while you are dragging on the screen, the shape of the box freezes but you can move it around the screen with your mouse.
PRESS SHIFT + COMMAND + 4 + SPACEBAR – This will take a picture of a window or open menu. [11]

The default way that Mac saves picture you take a screen capture is in PNG format. What if you would prefer the default format to be JPEG or TFF or PDF. You can use a command in the UNIX Terminal Utility to change the default. Here is the way that you can do that.[12]

OPEN TERMINAL

TYPE **defaults write com.apple.screencapture type jpg**

If you want the picture saved as a PDF type **defaults write com.apple.screencapture type PDF**

If you Want the default type to be TIFF type **defaults write com.apple.screencapture type tiff**

Making the above changes in terminal will set either JPEG, PDF or TIFF as the default photo / screen capture format.

USE YOUR MAC'S ISIGHT CAMERA TO STORE NOTES

Instead of having sticky notes stuck to your monitor why not use your computer's built-in camera to take pictures of notes and store them for you in Evernote or another notetaking program [13]

Here are the simple steps to do this:

A.   Launch the "Photo Booth" application
B.   Hold your note up so the camera can see it and take a picture
C.   Move it to the desktop
D.   Drag the picture into the Evernote application where the optical characterization software will make the text searchable

CUSTOMIZE THE MAC LOGIN SCREEN

Just like we discussed earlier in the Windows section, you can customize your Mac Login / Start screen in a few interesting ways. One way to do this is to add a small, customizable message to your Mac's lock screen. It cannot be a long message, but this way you can put your own unique flair on the lock screen. This way every time someone logs on / off your computer, they will see the message you created. [14]

IN THE TERMINAL, TYPE

Sudo defaults write /Library /preferences/ com.apple.loginwindow LoginwindowText 'Your message"

(Replace "Your Message" with whatever short message you would like to show up on your lock screen)

To remove your personal lock screen message and restore the original defaults type:

Sudo defaults write /Library /preferences/ com.apple.loginwindow LoginwindowText ' "

MANAGE YOUR FONTS ON A MAC

Many times, the first thing people think of when it comes to personalization the computer is the start or lock screen. The farther you choose is only sometimes thought about. Perhaps he considered were you thinking about how to start a document in Microsoft Word or another word processor. It is important to where your fonts are stored in the Macintosh computer, how to access them and how to manage them.

On your Mac fonts are stored in what is called the FONT BOOK. This is essentially one of three possible locations where your fonts by be stored. Fonts are found in these specific areas:

1. Main system library
2. A user library
3. A specific applications own library on your system

TO VIEW A FONT

OPEN THE FONT BOOK
SCROLL THROUGH THE FONTS LISTED

CLICK ON THE BLACK TRIANGLE BESIDE THE FONT TO VIEW MORE INFORMATION
ABOUT IT

TO DISABLE A FONT

Open the font book
Select a font to look at its typeface
GO TO EDIT > disable

Occasionally as you are adding and changing fonts it is possible to have duplicate
entries for the same font in your font book. When this happens, here's the remedy:

Open font book
View the list of fonts to see whether there are any yellow triangles beside them
(Yellow triangles indicate duplicate font entries
Click "Resolve automatically" to remove these duplicate fonts with one click. [15]
(No one wants a messy or disorganized font book)

The statement in parentheses above is what passes as this author's attempt at
humour.

Along with choosing and managing your font collection it is important for desktop as
sparse as possible this includes both minimizing the installed applications on your
system and removing any that you no longer use. The usual way applications are
removed from the Macintosh computer is simply to drag the application icon into the
trashcan on the desktop. There are three possible ways that an application can be
removed from a Mac. The three ways are:

1. Drag to the system trash
2. Removed using the uninstaller included with the application
3. Use an application uninstaller program such as App Cleaner, AppZap or
    CleanMyMac

Maintenance on any modern computer is generally less complicated in the past. While
some things can still be accomplished manually like removing cookies and deleting an
Internet cache, there are various programs that automate maintenance and cleanup
tasks on the computer.   Examples of these types of programs would include OnyX

and Tinker Tool. (https://www.titanium-software.fr/en/onyx.html and https://www.bresink.com/osx/TinkerTool.html)

There are other Mac Maintenance tools, but these are too of the most widely known.

In general, very little maintenance is required on Mac. There are a couple of things to do routinely on occasional basis. This includes repairing disk permissions, possibly defragmenting a conventional spinning disk, deleting corrupt preference files and repairing a disk drive. Let's look at each of these briefly.

Occasionally, over time this can develop bad sectors and develop defects. You can use the Disk Utility (Included in the utilities folder on your mac) to remedy this problem.

Simply open the disk utility
Locate your main hard drive on the panel on the left
Click on the "First Aid" tab
Begin the repair procedure (This could take several minutes to complete)

DEFRAGGING YOUR HARD DISK

Many people today believe that defragmenting a computer's hard drive is no longer necessary. Applications are coming continually being written and deleted from your computer's hard drive. The result is a possible fragmentation of files as they spread over different locations on hard drive. Some large files might be split into a couple of different locations in the drive. Some people think you do not need to defragment drive running OS X. Other than wear on the drive, there is no harm in performing this procedure. There is no need of lab included pneumatic for doing this. There are several third-party apps available for this purpose. You may want to look at iDefrag. You can find this application at http://www.coriolis-systems.com/iDefrag.php It is an application recommended by Randy B. Singer, the author of The Macintosh Bible [16]

DELETING CORRUPT PREFERENCE FILES

A preference file is a file that tells a program specific information about how to operate. If these files become corrupt or damaged, problems can occur. There is a simple fix

GO TO HOME DIRECTORY /LIBRARY/PREFERENCES

SCROLL THROUGH THE PREFERENCES UNTIL YOU FIND A FILE FOR THE APP WITH .plist AT THE END OF IT
Trash the file and restart the application

These are some simple ways that you can keep Apple Computer running smoothly with as few problems as possible. Your computer, especially one manufactured by Apple, is a big investment. Performing routine maintenance tasks like those mentioned above, is a small price to pay for worry free computing. It is likely that even without doing any of these things your Apple Computer will perform flawlessly. There are some people who never do any of these things and experience to little or no difficulties, but why take the chance, especially when, with a small investment of your time, you can virtually guarantee peak performance minimal effort. When problems do develop, they can usually be mitigated by repairing the permissions on the desk or performing a force quit on a program that has become frozen. In the unlikely event that your Mac won't start, what do you do? Have a checklist fire machine that includes the following steps:

THING TO TRY WHEN YOUR APPLE COMPUTER JUST WILL NOT START

1. Unplug everything except for the keyboard and mouse
2. third-party RAM may have failed, so try removing it (A black screen with three beeps usually means faulty RAM)
3. try to start up in safe mode (You do this by holding them the shift key as the Mac starts)
4. Reset the Parameter RAM (PRAM) by holding down for keys at the same time. Hold down COMMAND + OPTION + P + R keys. After you press these keys simultaneously, we hear the chime sound in the screen go black.
5. Start up in Single User Mode – you do this by holding down the COMMAND + S Keys as the computer starts. If you are successful you will see a command prompt after the computer starts in single user mode. When you see this UNIX prompt type **/sbin/fsck/ -y** the utility will then report any problems that it discovers
6. if your machine is an older one, try restarting from the OS X installer disk. (Insert the DVD into the drive and hold down the C as you start the Mac) if you can boot from this DVD, you can use the disk utility and repair the drive.

If none of these steps work, then you must reinstall OS X. This will not happen very often, but when it does, it is good to know the things you can try. [17]

When your Apple Computer does start up may suddenly realize you forgot something either at home or at work. In those situations, it's handy to be able to access computer remotely. On the Mac is very easy to do. You may not know this but included with the Mac OS is a service called "Back to My Mac". It allows you to be in one location on the computer and access your files from another location (virtually anywhere in the world that there is Internet access). This way, if you forget an important file for work at home, if you have your computer turned on this service initialized before hand, you can access this file even downloaded onto another computer remotely. To use the service, follow these simple steps:

1. GO TO THE APPLE MENU > SYSTEM PREFERENCES > iCloud
2. SCROLL DOWN UNTIL YOU SEE "Back to my Mac". (Make certain that "Back to My Mac" is checked in the box you see there)
3. You should now see the remote Mac listed in the sidebar under "shared"
4. CLICK ON YOUR REMOTE MAC AND YOU WILL SEE FOLDERS
5. CLICK ON THE FOPLDER THAT YOU WISH TO CONNECT TO

This is a very useful feature. It is puzzling then that Apple decided to drop this iCloud feature beginning with Mac OS Mojave (10.14). However, Apple users using OS X 10.13 and under will still be able to access and use this feature.

For those users currently on Mac OS Mojave and above, Apple recommends using the Apple Remote Desktop app or screen sharing in order to achieve similar results.

Accessing computer remotely can also be achieved by using VNC Remote Desktop.

VNC Remote Desktop is free to download and use for non-commercial purposes.

This is the VNC Remote Desktop website. To use this fantastic free resource all you have to do is visit their website at www.realvnc.com , sign up for a free account, install the application on any device that you want control remotely and go through the easy set up process .

The VMC Remote Desktop viewer allows you to see your remote computer from any other computer character to the Internet. You can access files, download remote files to your computer and control the remote device from anywhere there is Internet access. This allows you to be anywhere worldwide and still have access to another computer. Using this application, you can control that computer as if you were sitting in front of it. It is like the Mac feature described called "Back to my Mac" but Real VNC has applications for every platform imaginable including iOS, Mac OS, Windows, Linux and others. Be there even when you are not, use VNC Remote Desktop today.

In addition to Remote Desktop features another important thing you can do with your Macintosh is to save webpages for later viewing. In Safari you can do this simply by:

OPEN SAFARI

GO TO THE WEBPAGE THAT YOU WANT TO SAVE

GO TO BOOKMASKS > ADD TO READING LIST

THE KEYBOARD SHORTCUT FOR THIS IS **SHIFT + OPTION + D** [18]

You may see something on a webpage that you cannot take time to look at now presently, which would like to be easily able to find later. By saving webpages on the reading list in the Safari browser (or any other browser for that matter), you can easily go back and look at that webpage whenever you have time.

PRINTING SHORTCUTS AND IMPROVEMENTS

if you routinely print in a specific way you can set up user pre-sets. To do this:

1. GO TO PRINT > DETAILED PRINT DILOG BOX

2. ENTER ALL THE PRESET SETTINGS YOU WANT TO USE
3. CLICK SAVE
4. NAME YOUR PRESET

Here's another useful tip. When you print using Mac, you are most often given the simplified print dialog box if you want to change these options you must click on the show details option at the bottom of the dialog box. Barry will be presented with options to change such as layout, page range, color and quality of the print job. If you want to immediately start with the detailed print dialog box, you can once again change this using a few keystrokes in the Terminal application.[19]

OPEN YHE TERMINAL APPLICATION AND TYPE:

**Defaults write NSGlobalDomain
PMPrintingExpandedStateForPrint -bool true**

Typing these commands into the terminal will mean that any time you select print, you will immediately be taken to the expanded print dialog box instead of the simplified one that is the default. This can be very handy need to change options in the print dialog box frequently.

You can make the expanded print dialog box on a Mac default easily. As explained on the previous page, you can set the expanded print dialog pages default by entering a couple of commands in the terminal utility. The expanded print dialog box makes it easy to set specific options such as page layout, number of pages printed, paper orientation -- landscape or portrait and other things.

As you can see in the picture above, I use a Canon image Class laser printer most often, so the default is set to Canon MF 210 in the expanded print dialog box.

As you can see, there are many options you can adjust in the dialog box so that year print job will look exactly as you intend it.

PRINTER CONSIDERATIONS

Whatever you print, the way it looks on the page is only as good as the options you choose and the type of printer you choose. Many people choose a desktop printer as the printer of choice because they look at the cost of the device itself. What they fail to consider is the cost of printing. Cheap printers are available everywhere because printer manufacturers make their money on the ink or the consumables of the prefer to call it. The most common printer people by today is the inkjet printer. These printers can start as low as $29 but the ink they consume can cost anywhere from $49 and up

A better choice is a laser printer. Here is one that I use routinely call the Canon image class 217w. Here is the webpage dedicated to it on the Canon USA website

I show you this webpage because I believe that for the money laser printers offer the best value because they use toner instead of ink cartridges. Toner cost more up front than inkjet cartridges but toner last typically three times longer than typical inkjet cartridges. If you print a lot, you could buy a reasonably priced monochrome laser printer for approximately $79 and replacement toner will typically cost you around $49-$69 to replace. The cost per page on a laser printer is around $0.01-$0.02 per page whereas the cost on a typical inkjet printer is approximately $0.10 per page.

Also, nowhere is it written that you must buy toner from the manufacture it would like you to, but this will also cost you more than he needs to. Shop around and consider third-party resellers of toner cartridge. You can routinely buy 1/3 party toner cartridge that was to be caused between $1800 to buy from me original manufacturer for between 39 and $69.

What you buy is of course up to you, but it we shop around and consider cost per page and page yield that is page output when considering a printer.

ONE FINAL PRIECE OF ADVICE ABOUT PRINTERS

If you tell me, "No I don't print enough to justify the extra cost of a laser printer." Consider an Epson Eco-Tank printer

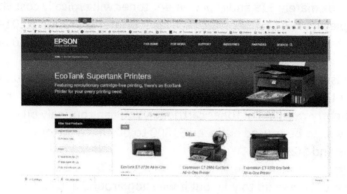

The Epson Eco-Tank printer does cost more up front, but these use lower cost refillable ink bottles. The Epson Eco-Tank comes with up to two years worth of ink right in the box (that's enough ink to print up to 11 000 black pages)

you should also be aware that toner cartridges for laser printers have a shelf life of at least two years. All these considerations mean that for me, and inkjet printer should be a printer of last resort. Further savings could also be achieved by searching in the printer settings dialog box on Mac and Windows foreign Inc. conservation setting. Different companies called the setting by different names, but it is typically found there. Turn on/enable this setting to conserve toner/ink even further.

PUT YOUR LAPTOP TO SLEEP BY CLOSING THE LID

some people believe that you need to turn off your laptop whenever you leave it for prolonged length of time. This is both correct and incorrect. If you are running your laptop on battery power, you should reduce key settings such as screen brightness and push notifications for naps because these can drain power quickly. Anytime you're not using a laptop that is running on battery power, turn it off when not in use

such as overnight or a prolonged absence of a few hours Closing the lid of a laptop such as the one seen in this photo as all that you must do when you leave it in the short term

Typically, you do not need to shut down laptop during daily use, but rather, simply close the lid. Closing the lid puts the computer to sleep and in the case of the laptop this is enough. Most laptops purchased today ship with a place to insert a locking table so that they can be left unattended without fear of being stolen.

SECURITY CONCERNSWITH A LAPTOP

you should be concerned about security on every computer, but doubly so on a laptop because the risk portability. It is an easy target for thieves and those who would like to spew your data can easily distill your laptop and access it at their leisure unless you have precautions in place.

Whenever you buy a new computer desktop or laptop make sure you enable Apple's "File Vault". File vault is Apple's built in hard drive encryption feature. When File Vault is enabled, the data on your hard drive is automatically encrypted/scrambled. This way even if someone steals your laptop, they cannot read the data unless they insert the correct password unscramble it. To turn on file vault go to:

SYSTEM FREFERENCES > SECURITY AND PRIVACY

CLICK THE PADLOPCK IN THE LOWER SECTION OF THE DIALOG BOX TO ENTER YOUR ADMINISTATOR PASSWORD

TURN ON FILE VAULT

BE SURE TO RECORD YOUR FILE VAULT PASSWORD IN A SAFE PLACE LIKE THE SECURE NOTES SECTION OF A PASSWORD MANAGER SUCH AS LASTPASS

IF YOU FORGET YOUR FILE VAULT PASSWORD, YOU WILL NOT HAVE ACCESS TO ANY FILES ON YOUR HARD DRIVE. YOU WILL NEED TO COMPLETELY ERASE THAT DRIVE AND RE-INSTALL THE OPERATING SYSTEM OTHERWISE.

OTHER WAYS TO SECURE FILES ON YOUR MAC

If you're concerned about security, and these days you should be, there are other ways to secure files on your Mac. Here's one example and how to do it.

Let us say you want to hide a file on your computer so that no one else could find it. That's easy to do –

Once again,

OPEN THE TERMINAL APPLICATION IN THE UTILITIES FOLDER

TYPE chflags hidden ˜ / Documents / hiddenfile

A file named "hiddenfile" is now hidden on your system

TO UN-HIDE A HIDDEN FILE

OPEN TERMINAL AND TYPE:

Chfags nohidden ˜/Documents/hiddenfile

CAUTION – IF YOU ARE GOING TO HIDE A FILE IN THIS WAY, BY SURE TO WRITE DOWN OR OTHERWISE REMEMBER THE NAME OF THE FILE YOU HIDE OR YOU WILL NOT BE ABLE TO RECOVER IT.

NOTE THAT IN THIS EXAMPLE, THE HAME OF THE FILE WE HIDE ON OUR SYSTEM WAS "hiddenfile"

In the command above, replace the word "hiddenfile" with whatever you wish to name the file that you are hiding.[20]

Encryption

Another way to grainy increase the security on your Macintosh and Windows machine for that matter, is to make use of what's called encryption. I've explored the subject of encryption in another book entitled "Encryption Simplified" published by Serendipitous Finds Publications, so I will not go into too much detail here, except to suggest that you should utilize public-key encryption (a common form of this is PGP with RSA standard ciphers. You can download PGP for Windows at
https://www.gpg4win.org/
once you download this program called "PGP Suite", you can use it to generate a public and private key, upload your public-key to public-key database such as key base at http://keybase.io and then encrypt all your sensitive documents so that only a person that you intend can read them. For more information about this, you can download the Kindle edition of my book, "Encryption Simplified" at

https://www.amazon.com/Encryption-Simplified-Maintaining-Privacy-Increasingly-ebook/dp/B07SVJZJ1W/

SECURELY REMOVE UNWANED FILES FROM YOUR COMUTER

When you delete a file from your computer whether it is a Windows machine or a Mac, is not really gone until that spot on the hard drive is overridden by another file. When UA click file and choose to delete, all it really does index marker to the file on the hard drive. There are third-party programs that can recover deleted files unless they are specifically overridden with ones and zeros.

So, if you want to securely delete a file from your hard drive, you should use the Secure Delete option on a Mac or a program like Erasure on a Windows machine.

On an Apple computer,

GO TO THE FINDER CHOSE THE UTILITIES FOLDER > DISK UTILITY > ERASE

YOU CAN SELECT A DRIVE TO ERASE SND ADDITIONALLY CHOSE THE" SECURE ERASE: OPTION

If you want to securely erase a specific file simply right click file rather than selecting "move to trash", chose "secure erase" from the list of available options.

On a Windows machine, download the program "Erasure' from https://sourceforge.net/projects/eraser/

REMOVE/ DISABLE MAC LOGIN / PASSWORD

perhaps you're the only user of the computer insecurity is not as big a concern for you. If that is the case, you can remove the logging requirement for your Mac in a simple way.

Open system preferences

click your name

click "change password"

if you already have a password to be asked for it in the OLD PASSWORD box

Leave the NEW PASSWORD box blank

Verify your choices

Your computer will not start up without asking for the start screen password

EMAIL SUGGESTIONS

When you sign up for things on the Internet and the company requests that you provide an email do not use your primary personal email address as this can lead to increased spam in your account. Instead, set up a temporary account on account meant solely for business/commercial emails. You could use a free service such as www.10minutemail.com These service provides a temporary email address and use for a short amount of time. Hence the name, "10 Minute email". Using a service like this allows you to give out distemper email and it remains active long enough for the website you interact with to send you a verification message. This is a message the company sends you that you must click on in order to verify your email address. Once you have interacted with this company and you have what you need you can abandon the email address and it will expire.[21] This is important because it minimizes your exposure because these commercial companies cannot continue to use or sell an email address that expires or becomes invalid over time.

QUOTE A SPECIFIC PORTION OF TEXT IN AN EMAIL MESSAGE REPLY

In an email message it is also beneficial to know that you can highlight a specific section in your email and quote back that excerpt in your reply. If you highlight a section before you hit reply, your email program will place that portion at the start of your reply so the receiver knows what you replying about, that is, the specific thing you're talking about in reference to his or her email.

TABBED BROWSING

you may be the kind of person who likes to have multiple tabs open in their browsers as they look for things online and go back and forth between times. You can use the following shortcuts to move between tabs in your browser

OPTION + T on a Mac

CTRL + T on a Windows machine

THE LOGO IN A COMMERICAL / BUSINESS WEBSITE IS OFTEN CLICKABLE

people are often unaware that the logo business website is often a hyperlink back to the homepage. This can save a lot of time you want to go back to the beginning of the website -- just click on the logo and BOOM, you are transported back to the homepage of the website [22] This works on most commercial websites such as Amazon, Facebook or Flickr for example.

if you like a fast way to get to the address bar of your browser you can use a shortcut ALT + D in Windows or OPTION + L on an Apple computer or device.

TO FIND A SPECIFIC WORLD ON ANY PAGE

To find a word on any page, you can initiate a search by using the following shortcuts

CTRL + F on a Windows machine

OPTION + f on a Mac

One final thing that is handy stone on an Apple Computer is that you can bring up Apple's built-in dictionary by double-clicking any word you select in an online document. This is handy if you're not sure about the meaning of a word or how release to the context of give a given sentence.

Hopefully, you will found at least two or three things in this section that you either didn't know or might have forgotten. There are great many features in the Apple OS X operating system that we have not talked about here, but this will give you a starting point to explore more your own. Every effort is made to include unusual or surprising elements here. You may find yourself saying "Wow, that's interesting!" If you did, great. If you didn't, perhaps you will find something the next section that will appeal to you.

Mac Keyboard Shortcuts

There is an extensive list of Keyboard Shortcut from Dan Rodney's Website at https://www.danrodney.com/mac/ included here for your handy reference [23]

Dan Rodney's list of keyboard shortcuts is large. Although the shortcuts can be found in various places on the Internet, Mr. Rodney's list os categorized by the type of shortcut or shortcut category such as Menu, Dock, Dashboard and Spotlight.

SUMMARY

In this chapter, we talked about many different things with respect to the Apple Computer and its operating system OS X specifically.

We talked about things like:

- Mac specific keys
- The Font Book
- Security features and options on a Mac
- Customizing your Mac desktop
- Mac keyboard shortcuts
- Enabling File Vault
- Accessing your Mac remotely
- Hiding files
- Expanding the Print dialog box so that it is the default option
- Accessing Special Characters
- Using your Mac's built in dictionary

AND MUCH MORE.

Now, after considering some surprising features first in the Windows system and the Apple environment, we will move on to some interesting surprises with respect to social media --Facebook and Twitter

PART THEE

SOCIAL MEDIA

HERE ARE SOME SOCIAL MEDIA TIPS

THESE ARE APPLICABLE TO ALL OPERATING SYSTEMS BECAUSE THEY ARE IN-BROWSER AND IN SPECIFIC APPLICATION SUCH AS YOUTUBE, TWITTER AND FACEBO

HERE ARE SOME YOUTUBE SHORTCUTS THAT YOU MAY BE SURPISED TO LEARN

YouTube was purchased by Google in 2005. It is said that 400 hours of new content is uploaded to YouTube every minute. YouTube has become an amazing communications platform with millions of subscribers. Users and "Social Influencers" who make their living by creating videos that millions of people are interested in. Social media has become a huge industry where people buy followers on YouTube, Twitter and Instagram. There have been many problems reported in the media about issues with false news associated with each of these platforms. It is up to each of us to remain vigilant and skeptical about we read and see online.

Facebook, social media giant, with over 2 billion users worldwide.

KEYBOARD SHORTCUTS IN YOUTUBE

Just press these keys while playing YouTube videos to move forward, play, pause or mute a video during playback[24]

J - jumps back 10 seconds of the video

K – Play / Pause the video

L – Jumps forward 10 seconds in a YouTube video

M – Mutes I YouTube video

YouTube Video Screen Capture

Earlier in this book, keyboard shortcuts were discussed to speed up productivity, reduce keystrokes in general make life easier. Many people are surprised to learn that Facebook's onset of shortcuts for moving around the network.

Above is a sill of my personal Facebook account page.

You can use the following keys to navigate easily from within Facebook. Jest login to your own account and move around easily using these keys [25]

FACEBOOK SHORKCUTS

J - Tap to scroll from headline to headline in your news feed

58

K – Moves backward in your feed

L – Clicks the "Like" button for whatever you are reading

C – Moves to the comment box

S – Click the "S" key to share something

? – Shows you the Facebook shortcuts

HERE ARE SOME FACEBOOK BROWSER SHORTCUTS

Here they are for WINDOWS

(NOTE: ON A MAC PRESS CONTRIL + OPTION (Instead of ALT) + the number)

EXAMPLE: CONTROL + OPTION + 1

ALT + 0 FACEBOOK HELP SCREEN

ALT + 1 FACEBOOK HOME SCREEN

ALT + 2 BRINGS UP YOUR PROFILE PAGE

FACEBOOK BROWSER SHORTCUTS CONTINUED

ALT + 3 FRIRNDS LIST

ALT + 4 FACEBOOK MESSAGE INBOX

ALT + 5 FACEBOOK NOTIFICATIONS WINDOW

ALT + 6 FACEBOOK SETTING PAGE

ALT + 7 BRINGS UP YOUR FACEBOOK ACTIVITY LOG

ALT + 8 FACEBOOK'S FACEBOOK PAGE (The company's own page)

ALT + 9 FACEBOOK'S TERMS AND POLICIES

ALT + M START COMPOSING A FACEBOOK MESSAGE

TWITER HINTS

Twitter is a social Network. It is also basically an "information, news and microblogging service".[26]

Twitter is a curiosity. Many people do not understand it and the company has struggled for years to make a profit. The company only recently abandoned its arbitrary 140-character limit for posts.

Many times, news stories and first reported on Twitter before anywhere else.

Here are a few things you should know about the platform

TWITTER TERMINOLOGY

HANDLE - I Twitter username

@REPLY AND MENTIONS –

@REPLY - use when one person is having a conversation with another Tweeter

MENTIONS --any Twitter update that contains "@username" anywhere in the body of a tweet.

HASHTAG – Any word starting with the hash (pound symbol) Hashtags deal with topic and make it easier to find and follow specific topics on Twitter

For example, you use @username within a tweet when referring to specific Twitter users. All your Twitter followers are alerted to your tweets including @username provided the person who you mention isn't using a private Twitter account.

DIRECT MESSAGES – Private messages sent from one twitter user to another – also called DM's. Direct messages can not be seen publicly by others on Twitter

Previously, only people who followed each other send direct messages, but now the user can allow others who they do not follow to send them a direct message or they can still limit it to only people that they follow directly.

Here is a graphic showing various Twitter elements / Components that is from Susan Waters and Kathleen Morris' website, "The Ultimate Twitter Guide"[27]

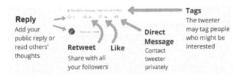

This graphic from "The Ultimate Guide to Twitter" shows the Reply, Re-Tweet, Like and Direct Message button /icons that you click on when using Twitter.

A direct message can be sent with the following format d@tritterhandle

A DM can also be sent by clicking on the "Message" icon in your Twitter conversation

Twitter, with its length limit encourages its use to be precise and allows people to skim through many Twitter posts quickly. People tweet about many different things, and, Twitter gain new popularity United States president, (@POTUS), The official Presidential Account. POTUS is an acronym. The letters POTUS are the first letters to each word of the phrase (P)resident (O)f (T)he (U)nited (S)tates.

The current president, Donald Trump tents to use TWITTER as a personal platform for whatever is on his mind, His now famous TWITTER handle is @realDonaldTrump Whatever the president his done or not done – regardless of your opinion of him, he certainly has helped to bring new popularity and interest to the social platform. As this interest is growing – it is worthwhile to know a couple of the basics for using it.

People tweet about many different things – some serious some funny.

First thing is that everyone on Twitter has a name. Many people use Twitter to follow famous people such as @TaylorSwift13 (Taylor Swift's official; account or Katherine McPhee (@katherinemcphee)

The "@" symbol (pronounced AT) represents a Twitter name or 'handle'

RT -Stands for re-tweet and is used to acknowledge something someone else said example: RT@stevenmilbrandt Climate Change Matters (This is only an illustration. In this example someone is re-tweeting a comment made about climate change

TWITTER BASICS CONTINUED

THE HASHTAG (#)

EXAMPLE; #Survivor Finale)

The hashtag is a label that people use to find things on Twitter

Example #Used Cars, #Canoe Trip,

Hashtags were originally just use to search for specific topics on Twitter

Today people just make up their own Hashtags and these may catch on – example #bestburger or any other topic they night conceive of, such as #nicestnationalpark

Some people have even started using hashtags outside of Twitter and regular speech. For example, someone might say in conversation, "Hashtag Yawner" or "Hashtag Amazing!"

This gives you a basic understanding of what Twitter is about so that you can begin to interact with it with some knowledge. If you're not sure what to tweet about, Susan Waters and Kathleen Morris offer these suggestions on their website "The Ultimate Guide to Twitter" [28]

What to Tweet About

Still not sure what you could be tweeting about? How about:

- A photo from a lesson (be careful using students' photos)
- A link to something interesting you've read
- A question about a topic you're interested in
- A request for a resource
- A link to something from your own blog or someone else's blog

- A favorite online tool you like to use with students

FLICKR (www.flickr.com

Flickr is a beautiful website where people can post their photographs for free

Yelp.com

Yelp is a review site contributed to by many. Recently their service came under scrutiny for the prevalence of "fake 'reviews, but this site remains popular because it is so widely known

HIP MUNK (www.hipmunk.com)

Receive Travel Deals and Exclusive Specials

FLIGHT AWARE (www.flightarare.com)

Get details of your flight status including delays and cancelations at Flight Aware. Well worth a look

Flight Aware offers many details that every traveller looks for when travelling

CRAIG'S LIST (www.craigslist.com)

The most popular "Buy and Sell" Website on the internet. Buyer Beware with any site where anyone can post anything for free.

GAS BUDDY (www.gasbuddy.com)

This site is amazing. Find the lowest price at the pump wherever you are. View the site on mobile for the ultimate in convenience.

OPEN TABLE (www.opentable.com)

Easy Restaurant Reservations. While not all restaurants are part of Open Table, many are. This makes reserving a spot at your favorite restaurant super simple.

These are some of the most useful websites on the Internet many you may have used before and others may be new to you. They make a useful reference or starting point for your web searches on various topics especially travel review sites.

PART FOUR

ADVANCED WINDOWS MODIFICATIONS

ADD MORE FONTS TO THE COMMAND LINE IN WINDOWS SHELL

The Windows shell is where advanced windows users can use the command line to perform specific tasks instead of the Usual Windows Graphic User Interface (WYSIWYG)

There is a way to add more fonts to the Windows Shell. Here is how [29]

1. First, you must use monospaced True type fonts.
2. Launch regedit and navigate to HKEY_LOCAL_MACHINE\SOFTWARE\Microsoft\Windows NT\CurrentVersion\Console\TrueTypeFont
3. Create a new REG_SZ and give it a unique number
4. Enter the name of the True type Font you want to use.
5. Reboot to make it available.

Again, if you are comfortable in the registry editor and want to add extra fonts to the windows Power shell, open the run dialog box by hitting the WINDOWS KEY + R as discussed in reference to keyboard shortcuts, launch the registry editor and make the above modifications.

Warning – only do this if you know what you are doing because incorrectly modifying your system with the registry editor can result in system problems.

Adding fonts to the Windows shell is not a necessary modification, but it does make working in the shell nicer.

WIFI SENSE

"Wi-Fi Sense" is a feature in Windows that allows users to share Wi-Fi hotspots that they find with their contacts and friends. This requires that the Wi-Fi access point be either open or shared using a key, but this provides a good way to share hotspots especially ones with exceptional signal strength with colleagues and friends. [30]

You can find out more about this at

http://windows.microsoft.com/en-us/windows-10/wi-fi-sense-faq

If your computer is fast, but you want to get just a little faster start-up speed, you can disable the start-up delay that Microsoft has turned on my default.

This involves a simple modification in the registry editor. Again, novice users should not modify the registry. Most people have no need to and would not appreciably benefit from the nominal speed increase that would result. However, it is a simple three line edit and a change in one numeric value. [31]

Here are the steps:

1. Launch regedit and navigate to CURRENT_USER\Software\Microsoft\Windows\CurrentVersion\Explorer\Serialize
2. Create a new DWORD named StartupDelayInMSec
3. Set it to 0.

Earlier in the last section of the book, personalizing the lock screen was discussed specifically as it relates to adding your own images. You will probably be interested to learn that the lock screen also has within it some hidden images that rotate and change regularly. If you want to see what these images are and perhaps save them to your hard drive, here is how you can do that [32]

1. Open Explorer and brows to
   %localappdata%\Packages\Microsoft.ContentDeliveryManager_[c
   ustom string of characters]\LocalState\Assets\
2. Copy all the files to a new directory.
3. Open a command prompt in that directory.
4. Run this command
   ren *.* *.png [enter]
5. Browse through them and find the ones you like!

PART FIVE

CONCLUSION

This book began with the assertion that the computer, with all its parts – motherboard, central processing unit, power supply, keyboard, mouse, and monitor, is both complex and simple. It's basic premise, that it operates logically with ones and zeros at its core, is a marvel and a curse. It has allowed us to do some amazing things, but it has also caused frustration and anger. Today, companies the world over, are collecting millions of data points on each of us every day. Most of us have no idea, who exactly is collecting this data, what they're using it for, or anything else.

For all our familiarity with the computer, it is challenging for what we don't know. Even the most seasoned professional, a so-called "technology expert" can only scratch the surface with what she understands because there will always be more -- more breakthroughs, more challenges, more amazing technology... More of everything in the field of technology to learn.

This book has tried to teach you some things you may not know regarding the personal computer, or as some call it, the personal confuser"

You learned –

- ✓ About some of the basic differences between the Windows and Mac operating systems
- ✓ about the phone book on the Mac and how it's used
- ✓ how to secure files on both the Windows machine and Mac
- ✓ you learned how to reactivate the hidden administrator account Windows 10
- ✓ a simple way to hide a file on the Mac a few terminal commands
- ✓ how to create hot key shortcuts
- ✓ the best value in printing
- ✓ how to activate and use the dictionary in on Mac OS
- ✓ how to use Remote Desktop in both Windows and Mac environments
- ✓ some social media secrets
- ✓ twitter basics
- ✓ saving webpages for later viewing
- ✓ private browsing
- ✓ how to customize the start screen
- ✓ how to use virtual desktops
- ✓ how to generate symbols and special characters
- ✓ The "Oops' shortcut keys

- ✓ What "God Mode" is
- ✓ how to create a one click shut down
- ✓ taskbar searching
- ✓ using Cortana to control your smart home

AND MORE

the author hopes you enjoy reading this book and that you got something out of it. If you did, you learned something. Great! If you are anxious for more, check out the bibliography of this book at the back and look for more titles by this publisher, Serendipitous Finds Publications. There are more.

Thank you for buying this book and investing in its author. Thank you to for reading it. There are many undocumented secrets on the Windows and Mac platforms. You have discovered a few in this book. You will discover more as you continue to use the computer and learn more of the amazing things you can do with it.

There are many things not yet invented that will astound and amaze you beyond belief. Never lose the wonder of childhood. Never stop trying to push yourself further -- to do and be more than you thought possible. Grow in little ways because small growth eventually leads to big changes and big changes made to monumental improvements, first to yourself and then others through you!

The person that you change may go on to change the world!

Believe in yourself and others well also

the author looks forward to sharing more with you... Come along for the ride!

BIBLIOGRAPHY

Dallas Thomas. "15 More Tips & Tricks You Need to Know to Master Windows 10." Gadget Hacks, November 20, 2015. https://windows.gadgethacks.com/how-to/15-more-tips-tricks-you-need-know-master-windows-10-0165984/.

———. "How to Easily Tweak, Mod, & Customize Windows 10." Gadget Hacks, August 26, 2015. https://windows.gadgethacks.com/how-to/easily-tweak-mod-customize-windows-10-0164082/.

Dan Rodney. "Mac Keyboard Shortcuts & Keystrokes | Dan Rodney." Good, Concise Mac Keystrokes, Tips and Tricks, 2019. https://www.danrodney.com/mac/.

David Pogue. *Progue's Basics: Essential Tips and Shortcuts (That No One Bothers to Tell You) for Simplifying the Technology in Your Life.* New York, New York: Flat Iron Books, 2014.

Drew Provan. *Mac Tips, Tricks and Shortcuts.* Warwickshire, United Kingdom: In Easy Steps Limited, 2012.

Faisal Hussain. "45 Tips & Tricks You Need to Know to Master Windows 10." Gadget Hacks, November 20, 2015. https://windows.gadgethacks.com/how-to/45-tips-tricks-you-need-know-master-windows-10-0163455/.

Jamie Harris. "5 Secret Windows 10 Tricks." BT.com, February 25, 2019. http://home.bt.com/tech-gadgets/computing/windows-10/windows-10-tricks-tips-god-mode-start-menu-11364201611969.

Jamie Lendino. "Windows 10: The Best Hidden Features, Tips, and Tricks - ExtremeTech." Windows 10: The Best Hidden Features, Tips and Tricks, April 13, 2017. https://www.extremetech.com/computing/191541-windows-10-the-best-hidden-features-tips-and-tricks.

Kevin Lee. "The Big List of 111+ Keyboard Shortcuts for The Most-Used Online Tools." *Buffer Marketing Library* (blog), May 20, 2014. https://buffer.com/library/keyboard-shortcuts-ultimate-list.

Manes, Casper. "The Top 33 Windows 10 Tips, Tricks, Hacks, and Tweaks." GFI Blog, February 18, 2016. https://techtalk.gfi.com/the-top-33-windows-10-tips-tricks-hacks-and-tweaks/.

Marain Cularea. "How to Unlock Secret Features in Windows 10." Windows Report - Windows 10 and Microsoft News, How-to Tips, August 6, 2018. https://windowsreport.com/secret-features-windows-10/.

Mark O 'Neil. "10 Hidden Windows 10 Tips You Probably Don't Know." Digital Trends, February 22, 2016. https://www.digitaltrends.com/computing/windows-10-hidden-tips-tricks/.

Marvin, By Evan Dashevsky and Rob. "22 Hidden Tricks Inside Windows 10." PCMAG, December 9, 2018. https://www.pcmag.com/feature/347136/22-hidden-tricks-inside-windows-10.

Mayank Sharma. "100 Windows 10 Tips and Tricks | TechRadar." 100 Windows Tips and tricks, May 11, 2016. https://www.techradar.com/how-to/computing/100-windows-10-tips-and-tricks-1307317.

"Nine Essential Windows 10 Hidden Features." *Smart Buyer* (blog), December 1, 2015. https://www.neweggbusiness.com/smartbuyer/over-easy/nine-essential-windows-10-hidden-features/.

Perschke, Susan. "10 Super-User Tricks to Boost Windows 10 Productivity | Network World." 10 Super User Tips to Boast Windows 10 Productivity, February 13, 2017. https://www.networkworld.com/article/3168427/10-super-user-tricks-to-boost-windows-10-productivity.html.

Stuart Yarmold, and Mile McGrath. *Windows 10 Tips, Tricks and Shortcuts*. Warwickshire, United Kingdom: In Easy Steps Limited, 2015.

Sue Waters and Kathleen Morris. "The Ultimate Guide to Twitter 2018." The Edublogger, October 15, 2018. https://www.theedublogger.com/twitter/.

The Unicode Consortium. "Alt Codes List of Alt Key Codes Symbols." Alt-Codes, 2019. https://www.alt-codes.net/.

WonderHowTo. "How to Use Caret Browsing." Gadget Hacks, July 22, 2010. https://internet.gadgethacks.com/how-to/use-caret-browsing-289253/.

Zac Hall. "MacOS Mojave Drops Back to My Mac iCloud Feature, Apple Remote Desktop Recommended - 9to5Mac," August 21, 2018. https://9to5mac.com/2018/08/21/back-to-my-mac-macos-mojave/.

ENDNOTES

[1] "22 Hidden Tricks Inside Windows 10", Evan Dashevsky and Rob Marvin, https://www.pcmag.com/feature/347136/22-hidden-tricks-inside-windows-10 December 9, 2018.

[2] "10 Super-user tricks to boast Windows 10 Productivity", Susan Perschki, https://www.networkworld.com/article/3168427/10-super-user-tricks-to-boost-windows-10-productivity.html February 13, 2017.

[3] "Windows 10 Tips, Tricks and Shortcuts", Stuart Yarnold and Mike McGrath, In Easy Steps Limited, Warwickshire, United Kingdom, 2012, P. 117

[4] "Windows 10 Tips Tricks and Shortcuts", Stuart Yarnold and Mike McGrath, In Easy Steps Limited, Warwickshire, United Kingdom, 2015, P.64.

[5] "Windows 10 Tips, Tricks and Shortcuts", Stuart Yarnold and Mike McGrath, ,In Easy Steps Limited, Warwickshire, United Kingdom, 2015, p.140.

[6] "The Top 33 Windows 10 Tips, Tricks and Tweak", Casper Manes, Tech Talk, https://techtalk.gfi.com/the-top-33-windows-10-tips-tricks-hacks-and-tweaks/ February 18, 2016.

[7] "How to Go Dark and More: 10 Windows Tips You Probably Don't Know", Mark O'Neil, Digital Trends, https://www.digitaltrends.com/computing/windows-10-hidden-tips-tricks/, February 22, 2016.

[8] "10 Super-User Tricks to Boast Windows 10 Productivity", Susan Perschke, Network World, https://www.networkworld.com/article/3168427/10-super-user-tricks-to-boost-windows-10-productivity.html , February 13, 2017.

[9] "22 Hidden Tricks Inside Windows 10", Evan dashevsky and Rob Martin, PC Magazine, https://www.pcmag.com/feature/347136/22-hidden-tricks-inside-windows-10 , December 9, 2018

80

[10] "Progue's Basics: Essential Tips and Shortcuts (that no one bothers to tell you) for simplifying the technology in your life., David Pogue, 2014, p.122

[11] Progue's Basics: Essential Tips and Shortcuts (that no one bothers to tell you) for simplifying the technology in your life., David Pogue, 2014, pp..129-130

[12] "Mac Tips, Tricks and Shortcuts", Drew Provan, In Easy Steps Limited, Warwickshire, United Kingdom,2012, P. 49

[13] "Mac Tips, Tricks and Shortcuts", Drew Provan, In Easy Steps Limited, Warwickshire, United Kingdom,2012, P. 202

[14] Mac Tips, Tricks and Shortcuts", Drew Provan, In Easy Steps Limited, Warwickshire, United Kingdom,2012, P. 118

[15] "Mac Tips, Tricks and Shortcuts", Drew Provan, In Easy Steps Limited, Warwickshire, United Kingdom,2012, PP.112-114

[16] "Mac Tips, Tricks and Shortcuts", Drew Provan, In Easy Steps Limited, Warwickshire, United Kingdom,2012, P.136

[17] "Mac Tips, Tricks and Shortcuts", Drew Provan, In Easy Steps Limited, Warwickshire, United Kingdom,2012, P 217

[18] "Mac Tips, Tricks and Shortcuts", Drew Provan, In Easy Steps Limited, Warwickshire, United Kingdom,2012, P. 84

[19] Mac Tips, Tricks and Shortcuts", Drew Provan, In Easy Steps Limited, Warwickshire, United Kingdom,2012, P. 103

[20] Mac Tips, Tricks and Shortcuts", Drew Provan, In Easy Steps Limited, Warwickshire, United Kingdom,2012, P. 25

[21] "Progue's Basics: essential tips and shortcuts (that no one bothered to tell you) for simplifying the technology in your life", David Pogue, Flat Iron Books, New York, New York, 2014, P.219

[22] "Progue's Basics: essential tips and shortcuts (that no one bothered to tell you) for simplifying the technology in your life", David Pogue, Flat Iron Books, New York, New York,

2014, P.253

[23] "Mac Keyboard Shortcuts: Good Concise Mac Keystrokes, Tips and tricks", Dan Rodney, https://www.danrodney.com/mac/

[24] "Progue's Basics: essential tips and shortcuts (that no one bothered to tell you) for simplifying the technology in your life", David Pogue, Flat Iron Books, New York, New York, 2014, P.287
..

[25] "Progue's Basics: essential tips and shortcuts (that no one bothered to tell you) for simplifying the technology in your life", David Pogue, Flat Iron Books, New York, New York, 2014, PP. 332-334.

[26] "The Ultimate Guide to Twitter", Susan Waters and Kathleen Morris, https://www.theedublogger.com/twitter/, October 2018

[27] "The Ultimate Guide to Twitter", Susan Waters and Kathleen Morris, https://www.theedublogger.com/twitter/, October 2018

[28] "The Ultimate Guide to Twitter", Susan Waters and Kathleen Morris, https://www.theedublogger.com/twitter/, October 2018

[29] "Top 33 Windows 10 Tips, tricks, Hacks and Tweaks", Casper Manes, Tech Talk, https://techtalk.gfi.com/the-top-33-windows-10-tips-tricks-hacks-and-tweaks/, February 18, 2016.

[30] "Top 33 Windows 10 Tips, tricks, Hacks and Tweaks", Casper Manes, Tech Talk, https://techtalk.gfi.com/the-top-33-windows-10-tips-tricks-hacks-and-tweaks/, February 18, 2016.

[31] "Top 33 Windows 10 Tips, tricks, Hacks and Tweaks", Casper Manes, Tech Talk, https://techtalk.gfi.com/the-top-33-windows-10-tips-tricks-hacks-and-tweaks/, February 18, 2016.

[32] "Top 33 Windows 10 Tips, tricks, Hacks and Tweaks", Casper Manes, Tech Talk, https://techtalk.gfi.com/the-top-33-windows-10-tips-tricks-hacks-and-tweaks/, February 18, 2016.